Old NEWTON STEWART

by
David Pettigrew

A 1931 view of Newton Stewart, showing, on the far side of the river, Minnigaff to the left and Creebridge in the centre.

THE VINERY 9 VICTORIA STREET.

NEWTON STEWART.

ACKNOWLEDGEMENTS

Thanks to James D. McLay; Rhona Wilson; Richard Stenlake and Denholm Reid for their assistance in the research; Ian McDowall for permission to use the picture on the front cover; Ross Cunningham for permission to use the photograph on the back cover; Robert Grieves for permission to use the pictures on page 33 and the inside back cover; Mrs Fox of Minnigaff; Mrs Murray of Galloway Granite Works, Sorbie; and Hazel Sisi of the Crown Hotel, Newton Stewart, for their help.

This vinery was behind the leather shop at 9 Victoria Street. Tanning and the manufacture of leather goods were once staple industries in Galloway. They were offshoots of the cattle trade which expanded during the eighteenth century and by the end of of that century most market towns had a tannery and leatherworks. The Newton Stewart tannery was located behind Victoria Street (at the Red Cross Hall). As local observer Robert Heron noted in 1792, it was managed with 'great judgement and sufficient success' and survived the economic slump of the early 1800s which caused Sir William Douglas's cotton mills to fail. It wasn't until the 1850s, when large city markets began to dominate the cattle trade, that the tanning industry in Galloway went into decline. The Newton Stewart tannery closed in 1870.

INTRODUCTION

Newton Stewart is not an ancient town and owes its establishment chiefly to developments planned and introduced by its landowners in the seventeenth and eighteenth centuries. There had been, however, tiny communities along this part of the River Cree since ancient times. Before 1700 Galloway was entirely rural and more or less cut off from the rest of Scotland. Its main settlements were medieval burghs such as Wigtown, Kirkcudbright and Dumfries, with the rest of the population collected in clachans and hamlets scattered throughout the region. Newton Stewart, Creebridge and Minnigaff all began as clachans, and each owes its existence to its position at a shallow point on the Cree.

Minnigaff was the earliest settlement. Roman and Celtic artefacts have been found in the area and tradition alleges that a battle was fought by Romans and Picts against the Scots on the site of Kirroughtree Park. There has probably been a church in Minnigaff since the thirteenth century, and the village that grew up beside it eventually became large enough to hold a regular market. This market may have been a stopping point for cattle drovers on their way to Dumfries; they would have crossed the Cree at a ford downstream from the village that connected Minnigaff Parish with that of Penninghame on the other side of the river.

From about 1400 the parish of Penninghame was the residence of the Bishops of Galloway, and in 1506 James IV passed through the clachan on his pilgrimage to Whithorn. Nevertheless, for two centuries the settlement consisted of little more than the parish kirk, two inns and a cluster of houses accommodating craftsmen and shopkeepers. By the mid-seventeenth century a fordhouse had been built, and along with the two or three houses around it, the little hamlet became known as Fordhouse of Cree. William Stewart, whose recently-built Castle Stewart stood nearby, was responsible for these buildings. According to one account, his new village was initially populated by 'the idle – those who hung loose upon society', but Stewart encouraged settlers with inexpensive feus and peasants who had accumulated a few pounds began to move in. In 1677 Stewart obtained a charter from Charles II promoting the village to a Burgh of Barony, and it officially became known as New Town of Stewart. The first three-quarters of the eighteenth century passed by without much further change, but by 1777 the population had grown to about 1,000, enough to require a new church which was built on the site of the present war memorial. By this time the influence of the Stewarts had waned and, seriously in debt, they had to sell off the estate. The buyer was William Douglas, a Galloway-born businessman, whose plans for the town ushered in a second period of development and expansion.

Douglas was of a strain of 'improving' landowners common in the period of Scotland's Industrial Revolution and he planned to create a manufacturing town that would transform the area's slow, agrarian economy. He renewed the town's lapsed burgh charter and then renamed it Newton Douglas, a trend he continued with Castle Douglas (and which earned him the derision of Robert Burns for 'new christening towns far and near'). His cotton mill, a large and expensive operation, opened in 1793 along with new houses for its 172 workers. These houses were grouped in Cotton Mill Row and the Gorbals (later renamed as King Street and Arthur Street). He also encouraged handloom weaving in the town, and an influx of outsiders arrived looking for work. Many were Irish, and even as late as the 1830s there were still enough for the town's contributor to the *New Statistical Account* to draw a distinction between the local Scots – who were apparently respectable and prudent with their money – and the Irish, who were 'little desirous of making provision for the future'.

After Douglas's death in 1809 and the demolition of his mill in 1826, the town reverted back to both its old name and an economy based principally on agriculture. Nevertheless, other industries continued to appear. Around 1830 bacon curing was introduced and proved to be 'a great benefit to the community'. In the 1840s there was also the extensive wool trade with the Yorkshire markets, handloom weaving remained strong until about 1850, and the town continued to hold an important district market. There was also the tannery, the brewery and a couple of grain mills. A number of local people also seem to have gone into business as publicans – in 1845 the town had as many as 34 pubs!

Just before the turn of the century Newton Stewart's fortunes seemed to be improving, and in 1899 a new mill was built on the site of the old one. In 1938 it was bought by Cree Mills Ltd. who concentrated on producing tweed and mohair products for a world-wide market (which included the Admiralty and several airlines). By the 1950s it had 147 workers, making it the town's biggest employer. The company was bought out in 1969 and the mill finally stopped production in 1986. The new century also saw the beginnings of tourism, and the railway started to bring in visitors attracted by the area's scenery and outdoor sports such as shooting and fishing.

Since the 1930s Newton Stewart has suffered a few blows to its prosperity – the railway closed in the early 1960s and an employer the size of Cree Mills has not settled in the town since they closed. However, there are plenty of businesses on the main street and a visit to the town on any day of the week reveals a bustling community going strong into the next millennium.

Minnigaff is separated from Newton Stewart, not only by its position within a different county (Kirkcudbrightshire), but also by standing in its own parish which stretches to the north and includes Glentrool. The village was probably established before the thirteenth century and there has been a church there since that time (there is a stone in the graveyard dated 1416). The ruins of a second church, probably dating from the seventeenth century, can still be seen in the grounds of the present one which was built between 1834 and 1836. Minnigaff had an established market long before Newton Stewart did, and a record of 1684 notes that it was of considerable size, held every Saturday, and 'frequented by the moormen who buy great quantities of meal and malt'. Old Minnigaff, which begins at this junction with Old Edinburgh Road, now consists mostly of houses built this century, although there are still a few that survive, much altered, from the eighteenth century. On the left, obscured by the trees, is the parish school which was built in 1907. It is now the youth hostel.

Minnigaff Village, Newton-Stewart.

Agriculture was the mainstay of Minnigaff. The *Statistical Account* of the 1790s records that sheep were the 'staple commodity', but adds that the land did not provide an easy living for the farmers, as is indicated by the archaic spelling of Monigaff which is Gaelic for 'stony moor'. Nevertheless, the parish's rural setting made it a reasonably healthy place to live and although the *Statistical Account* reported that the place was often infested with smallpox due to the lack of inoculations (a problem that would persist until the 1920s), there was one resident – still alive at the time of its writing – who was 118 years old.

Despite their fundamental reliance on it, there were a few opportunities for villagers to find work outside of agriculture. A corn mill was built or reconstructed in 1823 and in use until about 1900 (it later became a carpet factory owned by Blackwood Morton of Kilmarnock) and Cumloden Waulkmill was producing textiles from about 1800, remaining in business until the 1920s. Gathering oak bark for use in the leather tanning process was another important local industry and the parish supplied tanners throughout Galloway until the 1830s. However, there was little development beyond these and by the end of the nineteenth century the village contained little more than a dozen houses. After the Second World War it became clear that the land was no longer productive enough for farming so forestry became the parish's new staple. Glentrool Forest became a national park in 1945 and a village was built there to house the forestry workers. Minnigaff itself supported a sawmill until a few years ago; its site is now taken by an indoor bowling centre, private houses and Cumloden Manor Nursing Home.

GEORGE V. BRIDGE. NEWTON STEWART.

The George V Bridge was commissioned in celebration of the king's accession in 1910, although it didn't open until two years later. It was positioned over the part of the Cree known as Kirkpool, just above the horseshoe weir which was probably constructed to increase the flow of water to the wheels of Douglas's cotton mill (on the Newton Stewart side of the river). The bridge was paid for by public subscription and the opening ceremony was attended by over 1,000 people. A speech was given by Provost McCormick who was particularly proud that the bridge could be opened free from debt. It was repaired and restored in 1982.

Creebridge, Newton-Stewart

Creebridge was once considered to be distinct from both Minnigaff and Newton Stewart, even though it was never anything more than a single street. It was, however, regarded by those who lived there as a community in its own right, a view borne out by the correspondent of this card who notes that it is 'a little village we go through on our way from Newton Stewart to Minnigaff'. In the 1950s, the suburb still had its own general store, inn and two hotels, one of which, the Kirroughtree Hotel, is now separated from its parent community by the recent housing which constitutes 'new' Minnigaff. This view is unchanged apart from the disappearance of J. McCreath and the building that housed his premises. This has been replaced by a modern house which sits rather uncomfortably alongside its much older neighbours. The lintel of the house directly across the road bears the date 1769 and the other hotel, Creebridge House, dates from the same period.

The old Tollhouse dates from the early nineteenth century. When the bridge was built it led on to the two main routes into Newton Stewart, the Old Edinburgh Road which, still signposted in Minnigaff, followed a south-westerly route over the moors from New Galloway, and the Old Military Road which passed through the town on the way to Portpatrick from Dumfries. The Old Edinburgh Road was a turnpike road (on which tolls were collected) dating from the early 1700s; the Old Military Road was completed later that century. This was the only military road built in Scotland outwith the Highlands and it is likely that the route utilised early tracks that followed the coast and avoided the moors and mountains inland. Some of the 'A' class roads in Galloway today follow the old turnpike routes.

CREEBRIDGE NEWTON STEWART.

The name Cree derives from *crioch* meaning 'boundary' and the river separates Kirkcudbrightshire from Wigtownshire and also the parishes of Minnigaff and Penninghame. The first bridge over the Cree at Newton Stewart was built in 1745 but this was swept away in a great flood in the early 1800s. A horse-ferry replaced it and in 1813 construction of the present granite bridge began about a hundred yards downstream from its predecessor.

EVICTED.
The Congregation of Creebridge U.F. Church—2nd July, 1905.

The 'Creebridge Eviction' was a small-scale eruption that was the peak of an esoteric religious dispute which rumbled on throughout the first few years of this century. This unsmiling group have good reason to be unhappy, as when this photograph was taken they had just had their church taken away from them. The roots of the incident lay in the Disruption of 1843 when arguments about patronage and other issues resulted in about a third of all Church of Scotland ministers resigning from the established church – the Kirk – and starting their own Free Church. (Creebridge Church was built that year to house the local branch.) The Free Church splintered into other groups in later years, the biggest of which was the United Free Church, formed nationally in 1900 by a union between the Free and the United Presbyterian Church. Unfortunately, this merger caused a certain amount of dissension within the ranks of the Free and some members refused to be involved. Instead, they chose to keep the Free going and, their numbers depleted, became commonly known as the 'Wee Frees'.

CREEBRIDGE EVICTION
U. F. CONGREGATION MARCHING FROM CHURCH TO HALL

Because they were in the majority, the congregations of the UF Church kept on meeting in buildings, some of which officially belonged to the Free Church. Understandably, the Wee Frees were upset at being pushed out. It seems that they went to court over the matter and eventually the House of Lords ruled that they could have their churches back. In Newton Stewart the UF congregation was none too keen to give up its home and felt obliged to make its feelings known. Placing an advert in the *Galloway Gazette* under the banner of 'The Persecution', they notified the town of their intentions, and the following Sunday they marched in protest from Creebridge Church to the McMillan Hall where they were to be based from then on (and where the Wee Frees had previously had to worship). This was just the beginning of their protest and a bitter wrangle continued until finally, two years later, they got the old church back. In 1929 the majority of the UF's members settled their differences with the Kirk and were absorbed back into the official Church of Scotland.

A parade at the foot of the Cree Bridge on the Newton Stewart side. Although a date or occasion for this particular procession cannot be traced, pageants, parades and carnivals were once popular community events. In the 1920s and 30s, historical pageants were particularly prevalent and one of the biggest turn-outs was for a 'programme of pageant and carnival in commemoration of Sir Walter Scott' in July 1932. The procession began at Bridgend in the early evening and up to 4,000 people lined Victoria Street to watch a 'stirring spectacle and stirring scenes'. After the procession reached Dashwood Square, the entertainment continued in the McMillan Hall with a 'gipsy sing-song', followed by a tableau of scenes from Scott's works.

During the late eighteenth and early nineteenth centuries, the nearest Newton Stewart came to experiencing the Industrial Revolution that was sweeping the cities and towns of central Scotland was in the developments and improvements of the entrepreneur Sir William Douglas. Born in 1745, Douglas was a Galloway man of humble origins who started his working life as a travelling peddler. Later, he went out to Virginia where he made his fortune, and although little is known about the nature of his business in America, it was successful enough to make him a fortune of £500,000. By the mid-1780s he was based in London and had started buying estates throughout Scotland and particularly in Galloway. Among these were Penninghame and Carlingwark and it was on those that, from 1790, he focused his attentions. He renewed Newton Stewart's charter as a Burgh of Barony and had it renamed Newton Douglas. This new identity was further complemented by a new industry – cotton spinning – and a five-storey mill was set up in 1793 on the banks of the Cree at a cost of between £10,000 and £20,000.

Arthur Street, Newton Stewart

Soon after the cotton mill went into operation, other associated industries sprung up in the town. Handloom weaving became prevalent, and a factory producing rough carpets was established. A result of this industrial expansion was a rise in the local population caused by an influx of outsiders looking for work. Much was promised by Douglas's improvements and for a short time it seemed as though Galloway might become a major manufacturing region of Scotland. However, soon after his death a general depression in the cotton trade caused the closure of the mills in both of his 'planned' towns and the impetus for growth was lost. Newton Douglas reverted back to its old name and function as a market town and its cotton mill was torn down to make way for a quarry.

DOUGLAS HIGH SCHOOL. NEWTON STEWART.

Samuel Douglas was born in Creetown, became a plantation owner in Kingston, Jamaica, and on his death in 1799 bequeathed £10,000 for the building of a school in Newton Stewart. Apart from setting out plans for the school, his will stipulated a somewhat eccentric dress code for the pupils: 'the girls to be dressed in white, with each a red ribbon sash round her waist, and her hair, in ringlets down to the shoulders to be powdered and to be adorned with artificial or natural flowers, and the boys to be dressed in green coatees, with white waistcoats, long trousers tied with ribbons above the ankle, and . . . to have a little green silk bonnet on their heads, set around with flowers'. Although a Schools Commission report of 1875 had complained of the 'extravagance and absurdity' of these conditions, Douglas's wishes were apparently carried out until 1890 when the school's intake became girls only (the boys went to the Ewart High School). In 1922 the two schools were amalgamated and based at Ewart High (which became the Douglas-Ewart School), and thereafter the old building (above) housed the public health department for many years. It became a civil defence centre in 1962 but is now derelict.

Left: An unedifying example of street entertainment from the turn of the century. The Galloway Arms is the oldest hotel in Newton Stewart and the building probably dates from the mid-eighteenth century. Another old establishment that was on Victoria Street was the Shoulder of Mutton Inn, which stood on the site now occupied by the cinema. This was the place where Joseph Train, the Galloway exciseman, archaeologist and antiquarian, and his friend Mr Broadfoot, the parish schoolmaster, met to write their correspondence to Sir Walter Scott in the early 1800s. Train was a friend of Scott's and had made him gifts of many of his archaeological finds. He also collected stories and traditional tales of the area and forwarded these to Scott, who used many of them as the basis for characters and incidents in his novels including *Old Mortality, Redgauntlet* and *Guy Mannering.* Train is commemorated by a tablet in McMillan Hall. *Right:* Willie Moffat (nicknamed 'Black Sheep') was obviously enough of a local character to have his portrait taken and then reproduced on postcards for sale in the town. He is pictured here reclining on the ornate fountain which was a feature of Albert Street until the 1940s.

Victoria Street, Newton Stewart, Scotland, (The Snow Storm of Feby. 1895)

The circular extension to the building on the left of this view of Victoria Street belongs to the Central Bar, which probably dates from the late eighteenth century and is still in business today. Here it is beset by a huge snowdrift, the result of prolonged bad weather in February 1895. A despairing report from an edition of the *Galloway Gazette*, dated February 9th, outlined the seriousness of the situation: 'Since Wednesday last Newton Stewart has been effectively shut off from the outside world, and there have been no means of communication except by telegraph . . . The railway company are no doubt doing what they can to get the line clear, but the puny efforts of the gangs seen at work seemed almost ludicrous in the face of the Herculean task which lay before them, and it is impossible to say when success will crown their efforts.'

"And tell us all our rows renew
Along the flowery banks o' Cree."
                    Burns.

The flowery Banks o'
Cree at Newton-Stewart,
Scotland, in midwinter
(20ᵗʰ Feb.y 1895)

They looks fine and
cool this hard weather

The storm raged until well into the latter half of the week and the reporter went on to write that the appearance of the town 'baffles description'. When the storm finally passed the snow was a minimum of two feet thick and some banks on the main street were up to six feet deep. Finally, the town council called together the local unemployed to clear a path from one end of the town to the other. However, despite these hardships and the wailings of the local paper, the winter weather did bring its pleasures, not least skating and curling on the frozen Cree.

NEWTON- STEWART TAR-MAC CURLING RINK.

Curling has long been popular in Newton Stewart, indeed the Penninghame Curling Club was formed as early as 1828. Over the years the club has occasionally faced the problem of finding somewhere to hold its matches. In the 1850s a pond was built for members to play on but its banks later burst, causing substantial flooding to the premises of a nearby tanner who initially claimed damages of £176, although he later accepted £50. Work on other ponds was started and then abandoned, but in 1860 the club settled on a site at Barnkirk where they played until the Stranraer Ice Rink was opened in the late 1960s. The 'Tar-Mac' curling rink (above) was maintained by another club, the Newton Stewart Tarmac Curling Society. Built in 1911 where the library is today, the tarmac area was flooded whenever there was freezing weather and between 1921 and 1939 an annual competition for a trophy was played on it.

VICTORIA STREET, NEWTON STEWART.

The town hall was built at Fordmouth around 1800 and originally had a prison block at the rear. Apart from serving the town council, the hall was also used in the nineteenth century by the Mechanics Institute and housed their library. More recently, the ground floor was used for shops but now houses the council's local offices. As well as being the main shopping centre for the Machars district, Victoria Street has always been something of a financial centre. Long-established banks still in business in the town are the Bank of Scotland whose building dates from the early nineteenth century (it was remodelled in 1879) and the Royal Bank of Scotland whose premises were built in 1873. There is also the Clydesdale Bank and at one time there were branches of the British Linen Bank (later united with the Bank of Scotland), the Commercial Bank of Scotland and the National Bank of Scotland (both of which later joined with the Royal Bank of Scotland).

The cinema on Victoria Street (not built when this picture was taken) opened in 1933 and is still going strong, a remarkable feat considering its rural location, the number of cinema closures in the 1980s and the current rise of multiplex theatres in larger towns. One of the most memorable occasions in the cinema's history was the visit in 1969 of the author Gavin Maxwell who was invited to introduce a screening of the film version of his book *Ring of Bright Water*. Although he lived in the Highlands, Maxwell was a Gallovidian by birth and was feted as one of the region's most famous sons. The visit was promoted by a half page article in the *Galloway Gazette* which was accompanied by a series of adverts placed by the town's traders. Most of these made dreadful puns on the author's connection with otters (who were the usual subjects of his books): 'Our Cream Cakes "Otter" Be Good' a local baker embarrassingly announced.

ALBERT STREET, NEWTON-STEWART.

After 1900 the growth of tourism led to an increase in the number of hotels in the town. In the 1930s there were about seven of them, including the Black Horse, Jerdan's, the Grapes, as well as old established ones such as Creebridge House, the Galloway Arms and the Crown. There were also around ten boarding houses offering accommodation and one or two temperance hotels for those not inclined to enjoy themselves! Visitors guides were published by the town council to promote the area and they certainly made attractive reading. One from 1930 even goes so far as to quote the opinion of Galloway's chief medical officer – 'Newton Stewart has good hotels, clean streets, and the most intellectual population in the south'.

A parade at Dashwood Square some time before the war memorial was erected in 1921. The Square was known as 'The Angle' until the mid-nineteenth century and was possibly renamed after a friend of the Earl of Galloway. The McMillan Hall was built in 1884 with money bequeathed by the McMillan sisters, wealthy spinsters who belonged to a family of local grocers. It was built to be the largest public hall in Galloway and became well known as a venue for local music festivals, concerts and drama, as well as taking over from the old town hall as the seat of local administration.

PRINCES STREET, NEWTON-STEWART.

The area of Princes Street and Dashwood Square was the location of both the original parish church and the town's first parish school, which was built in the eighteenth century. The earliest mention of education in the parish dates from 1696 but merely states that there was no salary for the schoolmaster. An actual school is not mentioned until 1700; this was probably at the clachan of Penninghame, moving to Newton Stewart around 1738 and finally settling in a building on Princes Street that stood opposite the 1777 church. In 1877 this building was replaced by the present Penninghame Primary School. Another long-established school in the town is St Ninian's which was opened around 1825. Princes Street is the location of the Rutherford Church which from 1909 was used by the UF congregation after their Creebridge church – the one they had managed to get back into only two years before – was demolished. In 1924 they found their final home in the church building on York Road. This had previously belonged to yet another group, the Relief Church, and is now the local museum.

Penninghame St John's Parish Church was built in 1841 in what became known as Church Street and in the early years of this century was joined by Ruskin Hall, a small corrugated iron building that belonged to the Boys Brigade. Apart from the removal of the hall and one of the houses opposite, and the advertising hoarding on the side of the house on the right, this scene is more or less unchanged today. The street remains quiet and tidy, just as it is here, although a guide to Wigtownshire, published in 1908 and roughly contemporary with this picture, surprisingly complained that it was the 'one place in Newton Stewart where neglect and untidiness are allowed to reign'.

NEWTON STEWART BOY'S BRIGADE. 20TH JULY. 1908.

The 1st Newton Stewart Company of the Boys Brigade pictured at their annual camp at Clerkington in Haddington (along with the local minister and his wife). The company was at camp for a week and visited the Scottish National Exhibition in Edinburgh on their way home. This had been advertised in the *Galloway Gazette* and amongst other attractions they would have seen the Palace of Industry, the Machinery Hall and some of the best military marching bands. They might also have visited the Exhibition Post Office where they could send home postcards stamped with a special exhibition postmark.

In the late nineteenth century people started to look to sport for recreation and in Newton Stewart various clubs were formed. As well as the curling clubs, there was the cricket club, the cycling club, and the bowling club which was formed in the 1840s. From the 1880s the cricket club organised athletics meetings and it is likely that this group were photographed at one. Events usually included the tug-of-war, football matches, obstacle races, running, cycling and hammer throwing. In 1892 the tennis courts opened, followed four years later by the opening of a nine hole golf course, in the policy fields of Kirroughtree which were then owned by Major A.C. Armitage, proprietor of a Yorkshire cotton mill. In his opening speech the major hoped 'that the membership might be largely increased' and with an eye on the town's female population he 'especially welcomed members of the fair sex', a remark that got plenty of applause.

The Ewart High School opened in 1864 and was initially administered in two parts, fee-paying and non fee-paying. The Rector's house took up the central part of the building; on the left was the free school (or 'Ragged School') for the children of the poor; and on the right was the fee-paying part, split into separate sections for boys and girls. In 1868 the school had 141 pupils but a report from that year was stinging in its criticism: 'The school is disappointing. It leaves an impression that there is more show than substance about it.' However, when the division between ragged and fee-paying ended in 1890 the school seemed to get over whatever problems it had had and henceforth began to earn a reputation as an 'excellent' advanced school for boys (the girls were now sent to the Douglas School). The eventual merger with the Douglas gave it the new name of Douglas-Ewart and although extra accommodation was built for the increased numbers a brand new school with that name was opened in 1971, itself augmented by a series of surrounding blocks in the mid 1970s.

Corvisel Road, Newton-Stewart.

The house 'Lynwood' on Corvisel Road was the home of Richard Park, the architect responsible for many of the town's landmarks. These included the memorial to the Earl of Galloway (erected 1874), Penninghame School (1876), the United Presbyterian Church (now the museum, 1877) and the McMillan Hall (1884).

RAILWAY STATION, NEWTON STEWART. J.P.M. SERIES

In 1861 the Castle Douglas to Portpatrick railway opened, roughly following the route of the old London to Portpatrick mail coach which ran for the last time that year. The new railway was a continuation of the line from London and was originally run by the Portpatrick and Wigtownshire Joint Railway Company, a combination of the major railway companies in southern Scotland, the Caledonian and the G&SWR, and two English companies, the London & North Western and the Midland. From 1875 Newton Stewart's station was also the terminus for the Whithorn branch line (which closed in 1950). The station closed in 1965, seriously limiting the town's contact with the rest of the country, and when the last train left crowds turned out to wave it goodbye. Today, the station area has become an industrial estate and all that remains are an engine shed and part of a platform. Part of the site has now been taken by the post office's sorting office.

In February 1910 a goods train of 15 waggons travelling from Stranraer arrived at Newton Stewart Station, halting at the platform for water. At some point on the journey the coupling on the sixth waggon from the engine had given way, but the driver continued on unaware. While the fireman was on the tender adjusting the water hose the detached waggons caught up and crashed into the stationary part of the train. The *Galloway Gazette* reported: 'The fireman was knocked down between the tender and one of the waggons. The driver found the fireman under the waggon, the wheel having passed over his head, death being instantaneous. The driver sustained a severe shock but the guard was injured in the crash.' Severe damage was caused to the platform and several of the train's waggons were telescoped and badly smashed – the noise of the crash was heard a quarter of a mile away. The fireman was William Currie who lived near Dumfries; he was only 24.

DUMFRIES, CASTLE DOUGLAS, NEWTON STEWART, STRANRAER.

CALEDONIAN

A Leyland Lion owned and run by the Caledonian Omnibus Company of Dumfries. The company, an amalgamation of five smaller firms which had been based in towns throughout Dumfriesshire and Galloway including Lockerbie, Dumfries and Stranraer, was established in 1927. It was able to run services such as this one that went from one end of the region to the other. Later, Caledonian extended its operation to include Peeblesshire, a move which brought it into direct competition with SMT who took it over in 1949.

An Ordnance Survey map of 1846 refers to Queen Street as Wigtown Row; other streets had equally localised names, such as Glenluce Row, which became Princes Street. The names were changed in the 1870s by the minister of Penninghame Parish Church who, possibly in a fit of patriotism brought on by Queen Victoria's promotion to 'Empress of India', appears to have decided that royal monickers for the streets were more appropriate.

NATIONAL RESERVE "ANNUAL" ... STEWART 22nd JAN 1912

The National Reserve was begun in the years preceding the First World War, and was a similar movement to the Home Guard of the Second World War. It aimed to prepare civilian men to defend their country in the event of a war and had many ex-soldiers and veterans of the Boer War amongst its ranks. Dinners such as this one, held in the Crown Hotel, were opportunities to spread the message of the movement and encourage recruitment. The district section of the reserve was started at Newton Stewart in June 1911, and by the time of this event 101 local men had joined. The dinner was also a chance for the reserves to meet with the local territorial force and army officers, and generally seems to have been a jingoistic knees-up with toasts to the King, protestations of allegiance to the Empire and renditions of the national anthem. The evening ended with a long speech by the chairman espousing the importance of maintaining a strong army and navy; badges of membership were also presented to new recruits.

Crown Hotel, Newton Stewart.

962/33

The town's auction mart was designed by William Agnew and built near the railway station in 1895. Markets are still held every Wednesday throughout the year (and also on Fridays once a month during the first half of the year and every week during the second half), with the main event being the annual tup sales which draw in visitors from all over Scotland. The Crown Hotel began as a coaching inn and, of course, has always been in a prime position to benefit from the market.

NEWTON-STEWART

A need for new housing in Newton Stewart was identified at the end of the First World War. At the time most of the town's housing dated from the late eighteenth and early nineteenth centuries. Most of it was built during the industrial boom brought on by the improvements of William Douglas, although in Newton Stewart he never lavished the attention on housing that he gave to Castle Douglas, which he practically rebuilt in a classically-planned grid of streets. Newton Stewart evolved in a straggling manner and didn't conform to any plan, and by 1918 many buildings were unfit for habitation. Between 1924 and 1951 284 houses were built by the local authority. Despite this, many of the original houses remained standing and in 1955 it was estimated that 18% of all houses in Newton Stewart were either unfit, condemned or empty. At that time it was suggested that the town could benefit from becoming one of the New Town developments that were then being planned throughout Scotland. However, with the benefit of hindsight, perhaps Newton Stewart should be glad that it avoided the curse of 1960s redevelopment that spoiled other places such as Irvine.

In September 1913 a group of six aeroplanes belonging to the Royal Flying Corps flew over Galloway on a trip to County Limerick from their base in Montrose. These were probably the first planes to be seen in this part of the country and crowds turned out to watch them as they followed the railway line to the coast. This BE2 (No. 225 of 2 Squadron), piloted by Lieutenant Dawes, stopped at Holm Park for repairs and local schoolchildren were allowed two hours from their lessons to go and see the flying machine. The BE2 was the first British military aircraft to be produced in any quantity. It had a maximum speed of 72 m.p.h. and a ceiling of 6,500 feet and was used in the early years of the First World War for reconnaissance of enemy positions.

NEWTON STEWART FLORAL FETE

Despite being the technological geniuses of their time, the invention of the bicycle eluded the otherwise resourceful Romans. Instead the bike had its origins in seventeenth century France, although it was not until 1839 that Kirkpatrick MacMillan of Dumfriesshire added the cranks, levers and pedals so integral to modern bike design. Over half a century of further development ensued and it was only in the late nineteenth century that bicycles similar to those of today went into mass production. (Bicycles were manufactured in Newton Stewart in the early part of this century by Murchie and Picken in their garage at the Bridgend.) Despite being overwhelmed by a succession of inventions such as the gramophone, the picture postcard, the illustrated newspaper and the telephone, the public took the new vehicle to their hearts and a craze ensued. Cycling clubs sprang up everywhere (Newton Stewart's was formed in 1894) and every local gala or fundraising day, for a year or two at least, had to have a parade of decorated bicycles.

"FOX HUNT" CLIMBING CURLEYWEE, 5TH APRIL 1911.

The countryside around Newton Stewart remains a focus for outdoor pursuits. On the back of a similar card to this, postmarked 1914, a sportsman has written to his son, 'You would have enjoyed it here with me amongst the rabbits, grouse, partridges and mushrooms on the hills last night . . . The place is very quiet, no-one seems to have much to do, but everything is clean, fresh and pretty.'

PENNINGHAME HOUSE, NEWTON STEWART.

Penninghame House is situated near to the ruins of Castle Stewart, four miles north of Newton Stewart. The estate became an open prison with capacity for 85 prisoners in 1954, a development that caused controversy in the town. Not unnaturally the locals were afraid that the inmates might cause trouble. From the beginning, however, the prison pursued a policy of arranging work placements for inmates in the area, and it wasn't long before a few became integrated into the local community and chose to settle there on release.

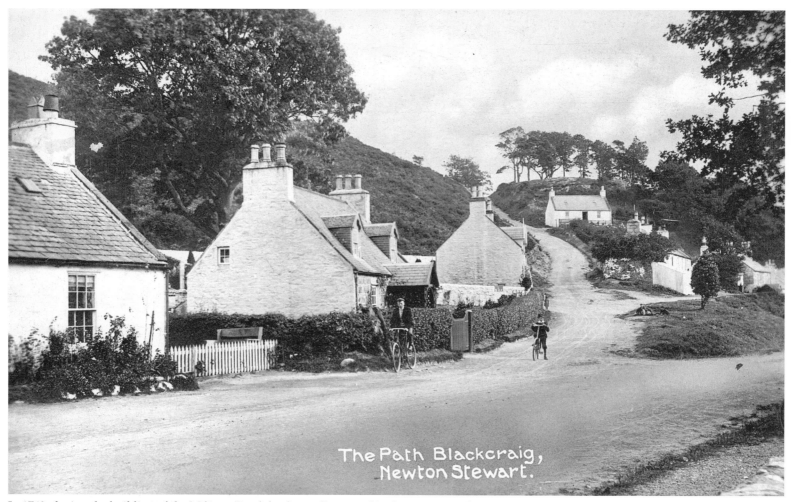

The Path Blackcraig,
Newton Stewart.

In 1763, during the building of the Military Road, lead was discovered in the area around Newton Stewart and the following year Galloway's earliest mines were established in Minnigaff Parish at Machermore and Blackcraig. The company responsible for the Blackcraig mines was the Craigtown Mining Company, a consortium of English and Scottish businessmen. They obtained both mining rights and permission for their workers to build their own homes near the mines from local landowner Patrick Heron. The mines at Machermore were operated by another company, perversely named the Blackcraig Mining Co.

THE ROADSIDE. BLACKCRAIG. NEWTONSTEWART.

By 1780 the Blackcraig operation was employing 44 men and was advanced enough to involve smelting kilns, furnaces and fire and water engines. Its position on the river just as it flows out to the bay allowed coal for the furnaces to be brought in directly by boat. Boats also transported the finished products of lead shot and bar lead to the London markets.

Blackcraig, Newton Stewart

Between the 1770s and 1790s the Blackcraig mines were at their peak, with the most extensive shaft reaching a depth of 25 fathoms (150 feet). The Craigtown Company was eventually wound up and the mines lay dormant until the 1870s when they were revived for a decade or so, this time employing 63 men and women. The last time the mines were worked was in 1917 (possibly to exploit what was left for the war effort) but this revival was brief. All that remains of Blackcraig today is the collection of houses on the hill above the road (as shown on page 42).

The A75 at Palnure in more tranquil times. In 1923 the village seems to have suffered a visit from one of those travelling evangelists who in the early years of the century plagued rural villages. The message on the back of this card reads, 'Visited this dear village Mon. Oct. 1st. Beautiful sunshine. Sang to the old lady in Post Office and read the 34th Psalm and prayed for her.' The message doesn't record whether the old lady asked for this or not, but hopefully she enjoyed the performance anyway.

PALNURE.

G.McM.

While no mining actually took place there, Palnure nevertheless owes its existence to mining in the area. Positioned on a creek which leads out to Wigtown Bay (Palnure translates as 'stream of the yews'), it provided a convenient harbour for boats transporting lead ore mined at Blackcraig in the late 1700s, and was later used by boats of the Kirkcudbrightshire Mining Company who from 1845 were mining the ore at Strathmaddie.

Palnure, Newton-Stewart.

Sloops of up to fifty tons could use the harbour, and at times traffic must have been considerable as more than 3,000 tons of ore were mined by the Kirkcudbrightshire company during the eight years that it was in operation. Meanwhile, those in the hamlet not involved in the mines or the harbour continued to eke out a living from farming.

Minnigaff Parish School was established in the 1690s and was located in Grovehill and Elmlea before it settled in Minnigaff village in 1907. In the 1840s additional schools for the parish were opened at both Bargrennan, and Stronord at Palnure (above). At that time there was also a charity school at Cumloden Cottage funded by Lady Galloway. This century another school was opened for the new community at Glentrool. The Stronord school closed due to falling rolls in the mid-1960s, and is now an outdoor centre.